Ideal Youth

By
Shaykh Mufti Saiful Islām

JKN Publications

First Published in July 2017
ISBN: 978-1-909114-26-5

British Library Cataloguing in Publication Data
A catalogue record for this book is available from the British Library.

Publisher's Note:

Every care and attention has been put into the production of this book. If however, you find any errors they are our own, for which we seek Allāh's ﷻ forgiveness and reader's pardon.

Published by:

JKN Publications
118 Manningham Lane
Bradford
West Yorkshire
BD8 7JF
United Kingdom

t: +44 (0) 1274 308 456 | w: www.jkn.org.uk | e: info@jkn.org.uk

Book Title: Ideal Youth
Author: Shaykh Mufti Saiful Islām

Printed by Mega Printing in Turkey

"In the Name of Allāh, the Most Beneficent,
the Most Merciful"

Contents

Introduction

All praises are due to Allāh ﷻ, the Absolute Ruler, the All Compassionate. May peace, blessings and salutations be upon our Final Messenger, Muhammad ﷺ, the Leader of Mankind and upon his faithful Companions and those who dedicate their lives through following their footsteps until the Last Hour.

The topic of youth has become a world wide concern, in particularly, for the Muslim community. The Muslim youth are responsible for their progression and development in the Dīn. The unfortunate sad state of affair is that not enough effort is being invested in this domain.

However, we must never loose hope. We must continue to develop ourselves so to not fall short in our responsibilities. By following the example of the ultimate leader, our Beloved Messenger ﷺ, we can produce a devout religious community of young Muslims with good potential and understanding.

This book contains articles gathered from various social media avenues; magazines, emails, WhatsApp and telegram messages, that provide useful tips of advice for those who have the zeal to learn and consider changing their negative habits and behaviour and become better Muslims to set a positive trend for the next generation.

May Allāh ﷻ accept this compilation and benefit us from the vital advices in this book. May He reward Shaykh Mufti Saiful Islām Sāhib immensely for all his efforts and bestow countless blessings upon his family and loved ones. Āmīn!

Palwasha Ustrana
Student of Jāmiah Khātamun Nabiyeen (Rotherham)
June 2017/Ramadhān 1438

Thirty Six Ways to Respect your Parents

May Allāh ﷻ give us the ability to follow these guidelines. Āmīn

1. Put away your phone in their presence.

2. Pay attention to what they are saying.

3. Accept their opinions.

4. Engage in conversations with them.

5. Look at them with respect.

6. Always praise them.

7. Share good news with them.

8. Avoid sharing bad news with them.

9. Speak well of their friends and loved ones to them.

10. Keep in remembrance the good things they did.

11. If they repeat a story, listen like it's the first time you've heard it.

12. Don't bring up painful memories from the past in front of them.

13. Avoid side conversations in their presence.

14. Sit respectfully around them.

15. Don't belittle/criticize their opinions and thoughts.

16. Avoid cutting them off when they speak.

17. Respect their age.

18. Avoid disciplining their grandchildren around them.

19. Accept their advice and guidance. Should their advice break any of Allāh's laws then inform them politely.

20. Give them the power of leadership when they are present.

21. Avoid raising your voice in front of them.

22. Avoid walking in front or ahead of them.

23. Avoid eating before them.

24. Avoid glaring at them.

25. Fill them with your appreciation even when they don't think they deserve it.

26. Avoid stretching your feet in front of them or sitting with your back to them.

27. Don't speak ill of them to the point where others speak ill of them too.

28. Always keep them in your prayers.

29. Avoid seeming bored or tired of them in their presence.

30. Avoid laughing at their faults and mistakes.

31. Do a task before they ask you to.

32. Continuously visit them.

33. Choose your words carefully when speaking to them.

34. Call them by the names they like.

35. Make them your priority over everything.

36. If they ask you a favour or money then NEVER say no to them.

Parents are treasure on this world and sooner than you think, that treasure will be buried. Appreciate your parents while you still can.

A Teacher's Great Example

A teacher asked her students to bring some tomatoes in a plastic bag to school. Each tomato was to be given the name of a person whom that child hates, so the number of tomatoes would be equal to the number of persons they hate.

On a pre-determined day, all the children brought their tomatoes well addressed. Some had two, some had three and some had five, some even had twenty tomatoes in accordance with the number of people they hated.

The teacher then told them they had to carry the tomatoes with them everywhere they go for two weeks.

As the days passed the children started to complain about the decay and smell of the tomatoes. The students who had many tomatoes complained that it was very heavy to carry and the smell was too much.

After a week, the teacher asked the students, "How did you feel this week?" The children complained of the awful smell and heavy weight of the tomatoes, especially those who carried several tomatoes.

The teacher then said:
"This is very similar to what you carry in your heart when you hate people. Hatred makes the heart unhealthy and you carry that hatred

everywhere. If you can't bear the smell of spoilt tomatoes for a week, imagine the impact of bitterness on your heart as you carry it daily."

The heart is a beautiful garden that needs regular cleaning of unwanted weeds. Forgive those who have angered you because this makes room for storing good things. Get better, not bitter!

Always Have Faith

Two beggars knocked on the door asking for bread. One beggar was given a loaf and sent away. The other was kept waiting and waiting. At length, the second beggar became concerned. "Why am I being denied? What is lacking in me that the other one was favoured over me?" he asked himself. Unknown to the beggar, a fresh loaf was being baked for him inside the house.

Let's remember that Allāh's 🕌 delays are not always His denials. His timing is always perfect. Allāh 🕌 has perfect timing. Never early, never late. It takes a little patience and it takes a lot of faith but it is worth the wait.

We do not know what tomorrow holds but know who holds tomorrow –Allāh 🕌, The Most Merciful, The Most Loving and The All Wise. Imām Shāfi'ī 🕌 states:

"My heart is at ease knowing that what was meant for me will never miss me, and that what misses me was never meant for me."

Look at the Positives!

An elderly Chinese woman had two large pots, each hung on the ends of a pole which she carried across her neck. One of the pots had a crack in it while the other pot was perfect and always delivered a full portion of water.

At the end of the long walks from the stream to the house, the cracked pot arrived only half full. This continued for two years daily, with the woman bringing home only one and a half pot of water.

Of course, the perfect pot was proud of its accomplishments. But the poor cracked pot was ashamed of its own imperfection, and miserable that it could only do half of what it had been made to do.

After two years of what it perceived to be bitter failure, it spoke to the woman one day by the stream.

"I am ashamed of myself, because this crack in my side causes water to leak out all the way back to your house."

The old woman smiled and said, "Did you notice that there are flowers on your side of the path, but not on the other pot's side? That is because I have always known about your flaw, so I planted flower seeds on your side of the path, and every day while we walk back, you water them. For two years I have been able to pick these beautiful flowers to decorate the table. Without you being just the way you are, there would not be this beauty to grace the house."

We all have certain flaws but it is the cracks and flaws we each have that make our lives together so very interesting and rewarding. You've just got to take each person for what they are and look for the good in them.

Ten Things We Waste!

1) Our Knowledge
Wasted by not practising it.

2) Our Actions
Wasted by performing them without sincerity.

3) Our Wealth
Wasted by using it on things that will not bring us reward from Allāh ﷻ. We waste our money, our status, our authority on things which have no benefit in this life or in the Ākhirah (Hereafter).

4) Our Hearts
Wasted because they are empty from the love of Allāh ﷻ and His Messenger ﷺ and devoid of peace and contentment. In their place, our hearts are filled with something or someone else.

5) Our Bodies

Wasted because we don't use them in Ibādah (worship) and service of Allāh ﷻ.

6) Our Love

Our love is misdirected away from Allāh ﷻ and His beloved Prophet ﷺ towards something or someone else.

7) Our Time

Wasted by not using it properly to compensate for that which has passed and by doing what is righteous.

8) Our Intellect

Wasted on things that are not beneficial but detrimental to the society and the individual and not in contemplation or reflection.

9) Our Service

Wasted in service of someone who will not bring us closer to Allāh ﷻ and nor something that will benefit us in this world.

10) Our Dhikr - Remembrance of Allāh ﷻ

Wasted because it does not affect our hearts.

Don't Insult Your Mother

Do we insult our mothers? Why do we need a special day to appreciate mothers? To honour our mother on one day which the world calls 'Mother's Day' is an insult. Mother's Day has become a nonsensical money-making farce that extorts hard-earned cash to lavish expensive gifts on our dear mothers, when in actual fact, the real gift should come from the heart and it should be done every day and not just once a year!

We need to arouse our sentiments and be conscientious of our obligations to our mothers, whose challenges and difficulties began prior to us coming into this world. From the very conception, our mothers were in difficulty. They bore us with pain, they delivered us with pain and they suckled us. The Holy Qur'ān says it took a great portion of two and a half to three years, of the strength, energy and ability of the mother, in this initial stage and the first development phase of our lives.

The love of a mother is unparalleled. Mothers are everything for us when we are small. Our lives revolve around them. There is no day that you are not duty-bound to your mother. There is simply no way we can ever really thank our mothers for all they have done for us. They are the ones who will be awake all night when we are sick, praying to Allāh ﷻ to make us well and be ever-ready to bear the pain that we may be experiencing. They are the ones to wake up early in the morning to make the nicest breakfast and endure all our tantrums.

So let us cherish our mothers every day and not wait a whole year to show her how special she really is. It takes someone brave to be a mother, someone strong to raise a child and someone special to love someone more than herself. Mothers hold their children's hands for a short while but they hold their hearts forever.

There are no words that can capture the emotion and the heartache when one loses a mother and the extract below best describes this.

Hello Operator, does Heaven have a phone number? Mummy went to Heaven, but I need her here today. My tummy hurts and I fell down, I need her right away.

Operator can you tell me how to find her in this book. Is Heaven in the Yellow Pages? I don't know where to look.

I think my daddy needs her too, at night I hear him cry. I hear him call her name sometimes, but I really don't know why.

Maybe if I call her, she will hurry home to me. Is Heaven very far away? Is it across the sea? She has been gone for a long, long time. She needs to come home now! I really need to reach her, but I simply don't know how. Help me find the number please, is it listed under Heaven? I can't read these big words, I am only seven.

I'm sorry Operator, I didn't mean to make you cry. Is your tummy hurting too, or is there something in your eye?

If I call my local Masjid, maybe they will know. Mummy said when we need help, that is where we should go. I found the number to my local Masjid tacked up on the wall. Thank you Operator, I will give them a call.

Every Day is Mother's Day

You must have heard people say that Muslims are different. One of the things that makes them different is that we do not have special days on which we do good deeds.

Every day is a special day for Muslims to do good actions. When we wake up in the morning, we should know in our hearts that we are going to be good. We are going to be nice to everyone no matter who it is. We are also going to be extra good and kind to our parents.

Being a Muslim is not just for one or two days in a year, but every day of our life. This is what makes us so special. From an Islamic perspective, the status of a woman, in particular, a mother is greatly honoured.

A man came to the Holy Prophet ﷺ and asked him, "Who is more entitled to my companionship?" He replied, "Your mother." He asked a second time, "Who next?" He replied, "Your mother." He asked a third time, "Who next?" He replied, "Your mother." Only after asking the fourth time did he reply, "Your father." (Bukhāri).

So this means that the mother, not only gets the gold medal, she also gets the silver and bronze one! The father only gets the consolation prize. Islām has given a mother three times more rights over her children than the father because of her important role in their birth, upbringing and education. Which other religion elevates a mother to such a status?

In another Hadīth, the Holy Prophet ﷺ said, "Paradise lies beneath the feet of your mother." (Nasai)

In other words, Paradise awaits for those who cherish and respect their mothers. Muslims are taught to love, respect, honour, support and cherish their mothers.

In Islām, Mother's Day and Father's Day are every day. Teacher's day, brother's day, sister's day, children's day, friend's day, neighbour's day, everyone's days are all, every day. In fact, all of these days are unnecessary inventions.

Allāh ﷻ has given us two celebrations a year; that is Eīd ul-Fitr and Eīd ul-Adhā. Shaytān looks for opportunities to create an innovation in religion. If we follow the Holy Qur'ān and the teachings of the Holy Prophet ﷺ, surely we can never go wrong. Let them guide us and illuminate our path of life for us.

My Dad

When I was...

4 years old: My daddy can do anything.
5 years old: My daddy knows a whole lot.
6 years old: My dad is smarter than your dad.
8 years old: My dad doesn't know exactly everything.
10 years old: In the olden days when my dad grew up, things were sure different.
12 years old: Oh well, naturally father doesn't know anything about that. He is too old to remember his childhood.
14 years old: Don't pay any attention to my father. He is too old-fashioned!
21 years old: Him? He is hopelessly out-of-date.
25 years old: Dad knows a little bit about it, but then he should because he has been around so long.
30 years old: Maybe we should ask dad what he thinks. After all, he's had a lot of experience.
35 years old: I'm not doing a single thing until I talk to dad.
40 years old: I wonder how dad would have handled it. He was so wise and had a world of experience.
50 years old: I'd give anything if dad were here now so I could talk this over with him. Too bad I didn't appreciate how smart he was. I could have learned a lot from him.

IF

If you can keep your head when all around you
are losing theirs and blaming it on you.
If you can trust yourself when all men and women doubt you,
But make allowance for their doubting too.
If you can wait and not be tired of waiting,
Or being lied about, don't deal in lies,
Or being hated, don't give way to hating,
And yet you don't look too good, nor talk too wise.
If you can dream and not make dreams your master.
If you can think and not make thoughts your aim.
If you can meet with triumph and disaster,
And treat those two imposters just the same.
If you can bear to hear the truth you've spoken.
If you can make one heap of all your winnings,
And risk it on one turn of pitch and toss,
And losses, and start again at your beginnings,
And never breathe a word about your loss.
If you can force your heart and nerve and strength,
To serve your turn, long after they are gone,
And so hold on when there is nothing in you,
Except the will which says to them, "Hold On"
If you can talk with crowds and keep your virtue,
or walk with kings nor lose the common touch.
If neither foes nor loving friends can hurt you,
If all men count with you, but none too much;

If you can fill the unforgiving minute,
With sixty seconds worth of distance run,
Yours is the earth and everything that's in it.

Four Things

A pious person once mentioned, "Four things are hidden in four, and found in four places:

1) **The pleasure of Allāh** ﷻ - This is hidden in the obedience of Allāh ﷻ and is found in generous people.

2) **The displeasure of Allāh** ﷻ - This is hidden in sins and found amongst the misers.

3) **Abundance of sustenance** - This is hidden in virtues and good actions and is found in the homes of the performers of Salāh.

4) **Constrained conditions** - This is hidden in disobedience and is found amongst the non-performers of Salāh."

The Success of a Farmer

There was a farmer who grew superior quality, an award winner in the corn production industry. Each year, he entered his corn in the regional competitions where it won honours and prizes.

One year, a newspaper reporter interviewed him and learned something interesting about how he grew his corn. The reporter discovered that the farmer shared his seed corn with his neighbours.

"How can you afford to share your best seed corn with your neighbours when they are entering corn in the competition with yours each year?" The reporter asked.

"Why brother?" The farmer replied, "Didn't you know? The wind picks up pollen grains from the ripening corn and swirls it from field to field. If my neighbours grew inferior, sub standard and poor quality corn, cross pollination will steadily degrade the quality of my corn. If I have to grow good corn, I must help my neighbours to grow good corn too."

The farmer gave a superb insight into the connectedness of life. His corn cannot improve unless his neighbours' corn also improves.

Those who live in harmony must help their neighbour and colleagues to be at peace. Those who choose to live well must help others to live well too. The value of life is measured by the lives it touches.

Success does not happen in isolation. It requires collective effort. So share the good practices, ideas and new knowledge with your family, friends, team members and neighbours and all. As they say, "Success breeds success."

Sayyidunā Abdullāh Ibn Umar ؓ narrates that the Holy Prophet ﷺ said, "The best friend in the sight of Allāh ﷻ is he who is the well wisher of his companions, and the best neighbour is one who behaves best towards his neighbours." (Tirmizi)

How Do You Know If You're Ready for Death?

Man's greatest fear is death.
We ask ourselves, "I want to know that if I were to die right now what would my death be like?"

Would it be painful, would it be pleasurable, would it be sweet?

Here is an answer:
Your death will be exactly as your prayer is to you right now.

Why?
Because when you pray Salāh what do you do? You go and meet Allāh ﷻ.
When you die what happens?
You go and meet Allāh ﷻ. If you dislike meeting Allāh ﷻ while you are in this world in the body, why would you want to meet Allāh ﷻ when you leave the body?

If Salāh is sweet to you right now, your death would be sweet, if you died right now.

If you eagerly wait for Salāh, then when death comes to you, you will eagerly wait to be released from this cage and soar to new heights. If your Salāh is a burden on you right now, death will be a burden on you if you die right now. If Salāh is painful, death will also be painful.

Safeguard your Salāh, improve your Salāh, and you will improve your connection with Allāh ﷻ because both of these are nothing but a meeting with Allāh ﷻ.

Ugly

Everyone in the apartment I lived in knew who Ugly was. Ugly was the resident cat. Ugly loved three things in this world: fighting, eating rubbish and love. The combination of these things combined with a life spent outside had their effect on Ugly.

To start with, he had only one eye, and where the other should have been was a gaping hole. He was also missing his ear on the same side, his left foot appeared to have been badly broken at one time and had healed at an unnatural angle making him look like he was always turning the corner.

His tale has long been lost, leaving only the smallest stub, which he would constantly jerk and twitch. Ugly would have been a dark grey, tabby striped-type, except for the scars covering his head and neck and even his shoulders with thick yellow scabs. Every time someone saw Ugly, there was the same reaction, "That's one ugly cat!"

All the children were warned not to touch him, some threw rocks at him, hosed him down and squirted him when he tried to come in their homes or shut his paws in the door when he would not leave.

Ugly always had the same reaction. If you turned the hosepipe on him, he would stand there, getting soaked until you gave up and quit. If you threw things at him, he would curl his lanky body around your feet in forgiveness. Whenever he observed children, he would come running meowing frantically and bump his head against their hands, begging for their love. If you ever picked him up he would immediately begin suckling on your shirt, earrings and whatever he could find.

One day, Ugly shared his love with the neighbour's dogs. They did not respond kindly and Ugly was badly moulded. From my apartment, I could hear his screams and I rushed to his aid. By the time I got to where he was laying, and sadly, Ugly's poor life was coming to an end.

Ugly lay in a wet circle, his back legs and lower back twisted grossly out of shape, a gaping tear in the white strip of fur that ran down his front. As I picked him up and tried to carry him home, I could hear him wheezing and gasping and could feel him struggling. I must be hurting him terribly I thought. Then I felt a familiar tugging, sucking sensation on my ear – Ugly, in so much pain, suffering and obviously dying was trying to suckle my ear. I pulled him closer to me and he bumped the palm of my hand with his head, then he turned his one golden eye towards me and I could hear the distinct sound of purring. Even in the greatest pain, that ugly battered-scarred cat was asking only for a little affection, perhaps some compassion.

At that moment I thought Ugly was the most beautiful, loving creature I had ever seen. Never once did he try to bite or scratch me, or even try to get away from me, or struggle in any way. Ugly just looked up at me completely trusting in me to relieve his pain.

Ugly died in my arms before I could get inside, but I sat and held him for a long time afterwards, thinking about how one scarred, deformed little stray could alter my opinion about what it means to have true pureness of spirit, to love so totally and truly. Ugly taught me more about giving and compassion than a thousand books and lectures ever could and for that I will always be thankful.

He had been scarred on the outside, but I was scarred on the inside and it was time for me to move on and learn to love truly and deeply. To give my total love to those I cared for. Many people want to be richer, more successful, well liked and beautiful, but for me, I will always try to be like Ugly. He always tried to give love unconditionally.

I Wanted to Change the World!

When I was young, I wanted to change the world. I found it was difficult to change the world, so I tried to change my nation.

When I found I couldn't change the nation, I began to focus on my town. I couldn't change the town and as an older man, I tried to change my family.

Now, as an old man, I realised the only thing I can change is **myself**, and suddenly I realised that if long ago I had changed **myself**, I could have made an impact on my family. My family and I could have made an impact on our town. Their impact could have changed the nation and I could indeed have made a change in the world.

I Made Sajdah But....

I remembered my grandmother's warning about praying Salāh on time. "My son, you shouldn't leave prayer to this late time." My grandmother's age was 70 but whenever she heard the Adhān, she shot up like an arrow and performed Salāh. I however, could never win over my egos to get up and pray. Whatever I did, my Salāh was always the last to be offered and I prayed it quickly to get it in on time.

Thinking of this, I got up and realised that there was only 15 minutes left before the beginning time of Salāt-ul-Ishā. I quickly made

Wudhu and performed Salāt-ul-Maghrib. While making Tasbīh, I again remembered my grandmother and was embarrassed by how I prayed as opposed to how my grandmother prayed with such tranquillity and peace.

I made Du'ā and made Sajdah for a long time. I awoke abruptly to the sound of noise and shouting. I was sweating profusely. I looked around. It was very crowded. Every direction I looked, it was filled with people. Some stood frozen looking around, some were running left and right and some were on their knees with their heads in their hands just waiting. Pure fear and apprehension filled me as I realised where I was. My heart was about to burst. It was the Day of Judgement. When I was alive, I had heard many things about the questioning on the Day of Judgement, but that seemed so long ago. Could this be something on my mind made up? No, the wait and the fear was so great that I could not have imagined this.

The interrogation was still going on. I began moving frantically from people to people to ask if my name had been called. No one could answer me. All of a sudden my name was called out and the crowd split into two and made a passageway for me.

Two angels grabbed my arms and led me forward. I walked with unknowing eyes through the crowd. The angels brought me to the centre and left me there. I lowered my head as my whole life was passing before my eyes. I opened my eyes but saw only another world.

The people were all helping others. I saw my father running from one lecture to the other; spending his wealth in the way of Islām. My mother invited guests to their house and one table was being set while the other was being cleared. I pleaded my case, "I too was always on this path. I helped others, I spread the word of Allāh ﷻ, I performed my Salāh and I fasted in the month of Ramadhān. Whatever Allāh ﷻ ordered me to do, I did it. Whatever He ordered me not to do, I did not do it." I began to cry and think about how much I loved Allāh ﷻ. I knew that whatever I had done in life would be less than what Allāh ﷻ deserved and my only protector was Allāh ﷻ.

I was sweating like never before and was shaking all over. My eyes were fixed on the scale, waiting for the final decision. At last, the decision was made. The two angels with sheets of paper in their hands turned to the crowd. My legs felt like they were going to collapse. I closed my eyes as they began to read the names of those people who were to enter Jahannam (Hell).

My name was read first. I fell on my knees and yelled that this couldn't be, "How could I go to Jahannam? I served others all my life; I spread the word of Allāh ﷻ to others." My eyes had become blurry and I was shaking. The two angels took me by my arms. As my feet were being dragged, they went through the crowd and advanced toward the blazing flames of Jahannam.

I was yelling and wondered if there was any person who was going to help me. I was yelling of all the good deeds I had done, how I had helped my father, my fasts, prayers, the Holy Qur'ān that I read, I was asking if none of them, would help me. The angels of Jahannam continued to drag me.

They got closer to the Hellfire. I looked back and these were my last pleas. Had not the Holy Prophet ﷺ said, "How clean would a person be who bathes in a river five times a day, so too does the Salāh performed five times a day cleanse someone of their sins?"

I began yelling, "My prayers! My prayers! My prayers!" The two angels did not stop, and they came to the edge of the abyss of Jahannam. The flames of the fire were burning my face. I looked back one last time, but my eyes were dry of hope and had nothing left.

One of the angels pushed me in. I found myself in the air and falling towards the flames. I had just fallen five or six feet when a hand grabbed my arm and pulled me back.

I lifted my head and saw an old man with a long white beard. He wiped some dust off me and I asked him, "Who are you?" The old man replied, "I am your prayers." "Why are you so late? I was almost in the Fire! You rescued me at the last minute before I fell in." The old man smiled and shook his head, "You always performed me at the last minute, did you forget?"

At that instant, I blinked and lifted my head from Sajdah. I was sweating. I listened to the voices coming from outside and heard the Adhān for Salāt-ul-Ishā. I got up quickly and went to perform Wudhu.

Knocking Nails

There was once a little boy who had a bad temper. His father gave him a bag of nails and told him that every time he lost his temper, he must hammer a nail into the back of the fence.

The first day, the boy had driven 37 nails into the fence. Over the next few weeks, as he had learned to control his anger, the number of nails hammered daily gradually reduced. He discovered it was easier to hold the temper than to drive these nails into the fence.

Finally, the day came when the boy didn't lose his temper at all. He told his father about it and his father suggested that he pull out one nail for every day that he was able to hold his temper. The days passed and the boy finally was able to tell his father that all the nails were gone.

The father took his son by the hand and led him to the fence. He said, "You had done well, my son. But look at the holes in the fence. The fence will never be the same. When you say things in anger, they leave a scar just like this one. You can put a knife in a man and draw it out. **It won't matter how many times you say I'm sorry, the wound is still there. A verbal wound is as bad as a physical one.**"

The Holy Prophet ﷺ said, "Anger is from Shaytān and Shaytān has been created from fire. Since water extinguishes fire, therefore, when one of you is overtaken by anger, let him make Wudhu."

(Abū Dāwūd)

In another narration it is mentioned, "The one who becomes angry while standing should sit down. If his anger has still not cooled down, then he should lie down." (Ahmad, Tirmizi).

The Holy Prophet ﷺ has said, "He who can overpower others in wrestling is not really a strong man. True strength is in that individual who can control himself at the time of anger." (Bukhāri).

Pride

Once a pious old man encountered a youngster who was walking towards him with his chest out and head held high. As he walked by the pious man he bumped into him, nudging him to the side. The pious man said to the youngster with a soft voice, "My son, please don't walk like that." With a furious and arrogant voice the youngster yelled out, "What!? Do you know who I am old man!?" The pious man replied calmly, "Yes my son, I know exactly who you are. Your beginning was from impure semen. Your ending will become a decomposed body and right now you are carrying urine and excretion inside you!"

Selfie

Squinching, teeging and smizing are all arts to selfie posing. If you do not know what a selfie is, I'd implore you to remain ignorant but this article might *cough* enlighten *choke* you.

If you have never heard the word, 'selfie', 'teeg' or 'smize' before, it means you are of a rare breed. It means you have not attempted to pout your lips into a self-induced collagen implant look, or gaze deeply into your Smartphone's camera while your jab arm extends in front of you and you mentally say "cheese".

Selfies are the new pics on the social network block with people taking photos of themselves and instantly sharing them on Facebook, Twitter and Instagram. We all have those friends constantly updating a display picture or avatar with their latest stroke of self-portrait photographic genius.

If you never thought you'd get that "up close and personal" with your friends and acquaintances' lips and other facial features, social media and the Smartphone has changed that forever. That's because in order to really enjoy it, you have to give in to it and become more transparent with it. Technology, the Smartphone and social media has made life about me, my selfie and I.

Turning the camera on yourself, while eating a double cheese burger is vain and embarrassing but amusing to your audience.

Mobile technology has made life easier but ironically has also made us antisocial and therefore intolerable and vain, therefore, somewhat obnoxious, lazy and therefore, less independent.

Because we're so used to getting streams of information at the tap of a few clicks, people have become more impatient and less attentive to what people have to say, rather than what they have to show.

There's something so fascinating about being able to communicate in badly spelt typeset that we'd rather check our emails and chat to people somewhere else on Snapchat or WhatsApp, rather than to physically engage with people and share the air we breathe, in front of us.

We're so hooked on to taking pictures of our food to instantly post them on our Instagram for friends, families and strangers to see. Our relationship is now all through electronic means by which we rather embrace one another than to actually physically carry it out.

Engaging with technology has become so addictive that it shares our pillow and has become the first thing we reach for in the morning. People are constantly on their phones and sometimes, in the most inappropriate places.

It's guaranteed that if someone gets to work or campus and realizes they're phoneless, they behave as though they've been thrust into a rehab centre called, 'the real world' for that day.

If you suffer from symptoms such as reaching into your handbag or pocket every five minutes for your Smartphone or you feel lost without your gadget, then you're an addict. And most of us probably are. While mobile phones of before might have allowed us to multi task because it only needed one hand to operate, Smartphones require both our hands and so much more attention.

Technology may be in the palm of our hands and has placed the world at our feet but it's made us aloof, cold beings, easily and constantly connected to a fake reality, disconnecting us from the reality that matters and changing the essence of our humanity.

Teenage Insomniacs

It is 2.30am. The lights are out, the curtains are drawn tightly shut and she's lying there, with a million and one thoughts running through her mind .... tomorrow's mock exam, scheduling a time for that appointment, preparing an outfit for the dinner next week. She tries to switch off because she knows she must sleep and yet, she can't help thinking about things. Perhaps a game of Candy Crush will help her to sleep or even browse through her messages (just in case anybody needs her urgently). But to no avail. Watch a movie and perhaps then fall a sleep. Instead she continues watching and eventually misses her Fajr Salāh.

Such are the troubled tales of today's teenage insomniacs. They burdened themselves with too many futile responsibilities and yet expect to attain top marks in the exams. They are in actual fact drowning so deep in an ocean that there seems no hope left for them in crossing it.

But wait - look to that lighthouse in the distance! Yes, that's the one, shining with the light of Du'ā. Yet the teenager wasn't still concerned about her Salāh. She didn't think that extra Tasbīh would help. She wasn't bothered about respecting her teachers- if they came late to lesson, surely they could tolerate her arrival just a few minutes later. Couldn't they?

While it may seem that these are only minor things, it is important to recognise that it is minor things that make up major things. My dear teenage insomniac: you cannot expect a restful night's sleep without devoting yourself to your five times Salāh. You will not ace your GCSE's if you intend to hold tight to your Twitter and Facebook accounts whilst studying. And you most certainly cannot achieve true contentment of the heart if your love for this world devours you completely.

It is often helpful to evaluate your Īmān; not once, not twice, but every day.

Is it really necessary to follow that fashion blog, even if it is from a fellow Hijābi? Doesn't beautifying yourself through, tenderly constructing your Hijāb and painting your face each morning quite defeat the purpose anyway? Is it essential to photograph and share every single moment of your holiday? And will comfort-eating really solve everything? While food may be a temporary consolation, it isn't an open invitation to health problems. It is stated in a Hadīth that 1/3 of the stomach is for food, 1/3 for water and 1/3 for air. And yet, what do we do? Fill it entirely, putting 1/3 down to being constantly 'starving', 1/3 as consolation-eating and 1/3 to merely being unable to resist temptation.

Although there are numerous medicinal remedies to insomnia, I can't help but insist upon recommending the one closest to hand: faith. In times of hardship, cling not to worldly dependencies, but your Dīn, for that is where you will find true strength.

So to all the teenage insomniacs out there, I urge you to cling onto that which will not lead you astray. Remember, it isn't about having the right mattress; it is about sleeping in the right manner.

At Least

Some say:
At least I try to pray a Salāh or two a day,
that way I know I won't go astray!

She says:
At least I cover some of my hair,
Oh whatever, don't judge me girl!
At least it shows I care!

He says:
At least I have a Topi on my head,
so what! No beard, pants low, spliff behind my ear,
but my identity I don't shred!

Others say:
Sure we fib and sometimes lie and we carry a tale or two!
but at least we don't go deep as most others do!

Most say:
At least we know we are Muslims and that's what counts,
it is on that belief to Jannah we'll mount!

The ignorant say:
We live in an age where we have to slightly
compromise this Dīn or else we won't be accepted.
We'll be cursed and treated mean!

I say:
O people, wake up and smell the Chai! (Tea)
Change your ways before you die!

Stop saying 'at least' and take account of your life!
and don't pin the blame on your husband or wife!
On that dreadful day when you shall rise up from clay,
brushing the dust, frightened you'll say:
O' my Lord! I am a Muslim
I believed in You so...
At least I accepted this faith from that of the foe!

Send me to Firdaus in Jannah, I want to dwell,
make my eternity, save me from Hell!

And Allāh ﷻ will say:
Well, Firdaus is for the righteous, who acted upon what I said,
for you My servant, you will lie in Hell's bed!

Once your punishment is over then you can enter Jannatul-Firdaus,
Until then you will have to cry and weep and show remorse!

But My Lord! how will I cope when I am led into Hell Fire?
And Allāh ﷻ will say:
Relax, O' My ignorant slave,! At least it will only be for a short
while!

By Shenaz Khan, Sheffield

Five Ways to Navigate your Parents' Rocky Marriage

Rocky marriages can be scattered with rocks and trenches for the husband and wife involved, but can be testing for their children. My parents, may Allāh ﷻ bless and have mercy upon them both, had a marriage that involved a series of disputes that I was too young to understand. Despite a number of counseling sessions with our local Imām and interventions with family and friends, the weight of many years of emotional wounds took their toll and their marriage gradually dissolved, ending in a divorce.

There is no denying that divorce is an unpleasant ordeal but there is reason why Islām allows it as a final resort after all other avenues of reconciliation and counseling have been exhausted. Divorce is only when it is absolutely necessary.

Navigating your parents' long rough marriage, temporary separation, or divorce can be troublesome, painful and confusing but you can train yourself to rise above this turmoil and find tranquility. As an adult, when I look back, I can say with assurance that the five points below really helped me and can do the same for you, whether you are a young individual who is currently experiencing your parent's rocky marriage, living with divorced parents or even parents who have remarried.

1. Trust in Allāh's ﷻ Will

Surrender everything to Allāh's ﷻ Will, increase your Tawakkul (reliance) in Him and you will never be discontent. Train yourself in trusting in Him often and accept what is written for you. Make Du'ā (supplication) to Allāh ﷻ to grant you and your parents only what is best in this life and the next and help you to overcome your difficulties.

2. Always Treat Both Your Parents with Immense Love and Respect

There are times that you may find yourself swayed towards siding with one of them, especially if you feel one of them has been wronged. Remember though, that your relationship with your parents was ordained by Allāh ﷻ and that you have to try your best to treat them both with respect and love. In the long run, instilling this will benefit your relationship with your parents and give you a sense of great inner peace.

3. Seek Support & Be Yourself

Speaking about your situation to a third party can be beneficial. A meaningful talk with a trusted friend can go a long way. If you feel your situation is especially difficult then seek professional help. Along with this, try to keep your own personal goals in sight so that you are not bogged down by your parents' situation exclusively. Strive to pursue goals in life that will bring both you and your parents' great happiness.

4. Be Grateful

Take time to frequently thank Allāh ﷻ for all the good things in your life. Thank Him for placing your parents in your life if you have both (so many people do not have this blessing and would do anything for a little more time with their parents), for a home, for food, water and a comfortable way of life.

5. Change Your Perspective

Strive to change your perspective when it comes to your parents' marriage. If they are separated or divorced and you have two different homes, then tell yourself, 'Two homes only means twice the love,' etc. A positive outlook can paint everything with a fresh coat of brilliance. One thing is for sure: there are a number of diverse family types and so many different challenges that one may face. Do not feel burdened, overwhelmed or helpless regardless of the situation and know that Allāh ﷻ will guide you out of this rocky terrain to a smooth rolling pasture.

Ummatī, Ummatī

Ummatī, Ummatī, our beloved intercedes,
Your doubts and desires, upon this the Shaytān feeds.
Don't be fooled by the devil's deception,
He can only tempt you through a false perception.

Abstain from sin as it could lead to addiction,
And enter Islām with complete conviction.

Unite, O' Muslims and put your differences aside,
Allāh ﷻ likes conformity so by His laws we shall abide.

We're different tribes and nations so that we recognise,
But we all stand equal in Allāh's ﷻ Eyes.

So love and hate for the sake of your Creator,
And with the right intention, your rewards will be greater.

It's easier to love than it is to hate,
Animosity and hostility will destroy your fate.
So open your heart and make amendments,
Allāh ﷻ loves you more than your family and friends.

Don't take this for granted and appreciate your Lord,
And pray that Jannah becomes your final abode.

Remember Allāh ﷻ because Dhikr is reflection,
May Allāh ﷻ cleanse our hearts and grant us all protection.

Truly the most honoured is the greatest in piety,
May Allāh ﷻ shower His Mercy upon our Ummah!

By Saara Kayani, Sheffield

Eighteen Sources of Barakah!

If we were to look for an Islamic definition of productivity, it can be summarized in the word "Barakah" or blessing. Being able to achieve more with few resources, doing much in little time, and generating a lot with little effort is surely a blessing from Allāh ﷻ. Yet, Barakah has somehow become a lost treasure these days; everyone's looking for it, but no one seems to find it!

You always hear people complaining that there's no Barakah in their time, no Barakah in their sleep, no Barakah in their money and the rest of it.

What is Barakah?
A well-known scholar explains it as follows:

والبركة: هي ثبوت الخير الإلهي في الشيء؛ فإنها إذا حلت في قليل كثرته، وإذا

حلت في كثير نفع. ومن أعظم ثمار البركة في الأمور كلها إستعمالها في
طاعة الله عز وجل.

"Barakah is the attachment of Divine goodness to a thing, so if it occurs in something little, it increases it. If it occurs in something much, it benefits. The greatest fruit of Barakah in all things is to use that Barakah in the obedience of Allāh ﷻ."

Sources of Barakah

I am a firm believer that Barakah is not a lost treasure but concealed from those who don't attempt to seek it.

Below will explain eighteen ways of attaining Barakah, the lost treasure.

1) Good Intentions

If you want something to have Barakah attached to it, then good intentions are necessary. More specifically, the intention must be for the sake of Allāh ﷻ. Looking again at the definition of Barakah, you may guess that without us intending what we have or do for the sake of Allāh ﷻ, the "Divine Goodness" won't be found in our deeds.

2) Piety and Belief in Allāh ﷻ

Allāh ﷻ says in the Holy Qur'ān,

"If the people of the towns had believed and feared Allāh, We would have indeed opened out to them (all kinds of) blessings from the heavens and the earth." (7:96)

Allāh ﷻ also says,

"And for those who fear Allāh, He prepares a way out. And He provides for him from (sources) he never could imagine." (65:2-3)

3) Putting your trust in Allāh ﷻ
Allāh ﷻ says in the Holy Qur'ān,

"And if any one puts his trust in Allāh, then He (Allāh) is sufficient for him. For Allāh will surely accomplish His purpose. Verily, for all things has Allāh appointed a due proportion." (65:3)

The Holy Prophet ﷺ said, "If only you relied on Allāh ﷻ a true reliance, He would provide sustenance for you just as He does for the birds. They fly out in the morning empty and return in the afternoon with full stomachs." (Tirmizi)

This concept of your limbs being 'blessed' and enabled to do good is truly a blessing and a Barakah we should all seek. It brings to mind a story of an old man who jumped a large distance that the young men were unable to jump. When the young men asked the old man how he did it, he replied: "These are our limbs. We protected them from committing sins when we were young, so Allāh ﷻ preserved them for us when we became old".

4) Reciting the Holy Qur'ān

This is the fountain of Barakah! But Subhān-Allāh, we rarely engage in it. Allāh ﷻ says in the Holy Qur'ān,

"And this is a Book which We have sent down, bringing blessings and confirming (the revelations) which came before it." (7:92)

So, recite the Holy Qur'ān daily and observe the blessings and Barakah of Allāh ﷻ entering your life. The further we are from this Book of Guidance, the less Barakah we will have in our lives.

5) Saying Bismillāh before Beginning anything

When you say "Bismillāh" before anything you do, you're invoking the name of Allāh ﷻ on that activity. Not only will that activity be blessed but Shaytān cannot take part in it! So always say "Bismillāh" before anything you do! Subhān-Allāh, it's easy for us to forget to say "Bismillāh". Sometimes we're so used to saying it that we cannot remember whether we said it or not! Try to be conscious of saying "Bismillāh" and understand what you're saying before you act.

6) Eating within a Group

Anyone who has had the experience of inviting guests to his/her house will know this. No matter how little you think the food you're presenting to your guest is, it's always more than enough!

Note: This is not an excuse to be miserly when you invite guests over; in fact we should follow the Sunnah of Prophet Ibrāhīm 🕮 whom when visited by the angels prepared a large meal for them. What I'm referring to here is the blessings that descend upon those who eat together as confirmed in the Hadīth of the Holy Prophet 🕮 who said, "Eat together, for there is blessing in the Jamā'ah (in a group or congregation)."

In another Hadīth, "Whoever has food enough for two people, should take a third one, and whoever has food enough for four people, should take a fifth or a sixth." (Bukhāri)

7) Honesty in Trade

This applies to all business people (including ebayers). Never assume that lying and deceiving people will bring profit in your trade. On the contrary, it will remove the blessing from your income. The Holy Prophet 🕮 said, "The buyer and the seller have the option of cancelling or confirming the bargain unless they separate, and if they spoke the truth and made clear the defects of the goods, then there will be blessing in their bargain, but if they told lies and concealed the facts, their bargain will be deprived of Allāh's 🕮 blessings."

(Bukhāri)

Yes, it's difficult to be honest when you're trying to sell something, but it is worth it in the long run.

8) Du'ā

Ask Allāh 🕮 for Barakah! If you take note of some of the Du'ās of the Holy Prophet 🕮 you'll notice that he used to make Du'ā for

Barakah. We always say, "May Allāh ﷻ bless you!" Well, guess what? That's a source of Barakah! Also, when you're invited to someone's house, the Holy Prophet ﷺ advised us to make the following Du'ā for the host, "O Allāh! bless for them that which You have provided them, forgive them and have mercy upon them."

9) Halāl Income/Money

The Holy Prophet ﷺ said, "O people! Allāh ﷻ is Pure and He only accepts that which is pure."

Scholars say this refers to Halāl income. Scholars have also said that if someone eats Harām, then his limbs will disobey Allāh ﷻ but if someone eats Halāl then his limbs will also do good and obey Allāh ﷻ.

10) Following the Sunnah of the Holy Prophet ﷺ in Everything

The most productive man in the history of humanity is our beloved Prophet ﷺ. By simply following his lifestyle and his Sunnah, which we so often hear about, we obtain a great source of Barakah. Some of these Sunnats include eating at Suhūr time, eating with the right hand from the side of the plate, licking your fingers after finishing your meal, sleeping on your right side, using the Siwāk and much more. Look out for these Sunnats and follow them to imitate the life of the most blessed man on earth is surely a source of blessing.

11) Performing Salātul-Istikhāra

Performing Salātul-Istikhāra in all matters and then leaving the out-come to Allāh 🕮 as well as accepting His Decree is a great source of Barakah. The Holy Prophet 🕮 taught us a particular Du'ā which helps us make the correct judgement and not regret the choices. It is related by Sayyidunā Jābir Ibn Abdullāh 🕮 who says that the Holy Prophet 🕮 would instruct us to pray for guidance in all of our con-cerns, just as he would teach us a chapter from the Holy Qur'ān.

He would say, "If any of you intends to undertake a matter then let him pray two Rak'āh of Nafl Salāh and thereafter, recite the follow-ing supplication:

'O Allāh, I seek Your counsel by Your knowledge and by Your power. I seek strength and I ask You from Your immense favour, for verily You are able while I am not and verily You know while I do not and You are the Knower of the unseen. O' Allāh! if You know this affair (and intend your need at this point) to be good for me in relation to my religion, my life and end, then decree and facilitate it for me, and bless me with it, and if You know this affair to be ill for me towards my religion, my life and end, then remove it from me and remove me from it, and decree for me what is good ,wherever it be and make me satisfied with such.'

One who seeks guidance from his Creator and consults his fellow believers and then remains firm in his resolve does not regret, for Allāh 🕮 has said,

"Consult them in the affair. Then when you have taken a decision, put your trust in Allāh." (3:159)

12) Giving Thanks to Allāh ﷻ in Abundance

Allāh ﷻ says,

"If you are grateful, I will add more (favours) unto you." (14:7)

A scholar once said that if one ponders over the Arabic words in this verse, it confirms that Allāh ﷻ will favour the person who thanks Him is actually in the form of an oath – **"La azīdannakum"**.

So Allāh ﷻ is promising the person who thanks Him an increase in goodness and blessings and Allāh ﷻ never breaks His promises.

13) Give Charity

In Hadīth Qudsi, Allāh ﷻ says,
"O son of Ādam, spend (in charity) and I'll spend on you!"

Whenever you are broke or you feel Barakah is extracted from your life and urgently need it to return, then the quickest way of regaining it in your life is by giving charity.

For example, let's say Barakah was removed from your life due to a sin you committed; charity cleanses your sins, adds a good deed to your record and removes calamity. The pleasure and Barakah that lies behind giving charity cannot be described in words.

14) Joining Ties of Kinship

Sayyidunā Abū Hurairah ﷺ relates that the Holy Prophet ﷺ said, "Allāh ﷻ created His creation, and when He finished it, kinship rose and complained to Allāh ﷻ whereupon Allāh ﷻ said, 'What is the matter?' It said, 'I seek refuge with You from those who sever the ties of kith and kin.' Allāh ﷻ said, 'Will you be satisfied if I bestow My favours on him who keeps your ties, and withhold My favours from him who severs your ties?' It said, 'Yes, O my Lord!' Then Allāh ﷻ said, 'That is for you.'"

Sayyidunā Abū Hurairah ﷺ added, "If you wish, you can recite (the verse); *"Would you then if you were given the authority then cause mischief in the land and sever your ties of kinship?"* (Bukhāri)

15) Waking Up Early

The Holy Prophet ﷺ said, "Allāh made the early hours blessed for my Ummah." (Ahmad)

Such gems of productivity are the sources of blessings which we should seek to make our life productive. Waking up early hours in the morning is an important step to being blessed and feeling good throughout your day.

Try to wake up for Tahajjud, and then work during the hours before Fajr Salāh. If you cannot, then at least wake up for Fajr and stay up till sunrise before you return to sleep. Those hours are filled with

Barakah. If you're able to go to work in those hours, do so, you'll get much more work done than the whole day put together!

16) Marriage

Allāh ﷻ says in the Holy Qur'ān,

"Marry those among you who are single and the virtuous ones among yourselves, male or female: if they are in poverty, Allāh will give them means out of His grace: for Allāh encompasses all and He Knows all things."(24:32)

17) Salāh
Allāh ﷻ says in the Holy Qur'ān,

"Enjoin prayer on your family and be constant therein. We ask you not to provide sustenance: We provide it for you. But the (fruit of) the Hereafter is for righteousness." (20:132)

To illustrate the point of Salāh further, just imagine how your life would be without this great act of Ibādah. Where would Barakah come from? Never neglect your Salāh because this is your daily nourishment for the soul and salvation.

18) Asking Allāh ﷻ for Forgiveness

The Holy Prophet ﷺ said, "If anyone continually asks forgiveness from Allāh ﷻ, Allāh ﷻ will appoint for him a way out of every distress, and a relief from every anxiety, and will provide for him from where he did not reckon."

I pray Allāh ﷻ grants us the ability to value and practice all of the above points, Āmīn.

Time, Slowly Ticking Away

Out of all things, the most daring thing that will challenge you days on end is time. It's daring because it's never at a standstill, it's daring because you will never keep up with it and it's also daring because you will not find a solution for it.

Praise is to Allāh ﷻ, the Most Kind and may peace and blessings be upon all of the Messengers whom Allāh ﷻ sent to this short lasting abode.

We all try to keep up with it (time), to the point that we end up exhausting ourselves to keep up with it.

Time is faster than us but to make effective use of it, chasing it is not the solution. It will otherwise exhaust you resulting inconsistency in taking full advantage of time.

As the sun rises at its appointed time, the cool breeze of the morning makes its appearance but when darkness comes, day light disappears. This continuation never stops, hence time never stops for anyone.

Taking you out on a typical Monday morning (on your way to work) when traffic is at its peak, the remarks are, "If only time stopped/or If I had the power to stop it (in this desperate time)."

After a few repetitions, you finally get used to waking up a little earlier, in time for the cool breeze. Now traffic is catching you. There is enough time in your hands and like normally said, when you have the upper hand on time, "I am ahead of time," though still, not in the real sense.

When a person utilises their time correctly, the outcome is pleasant like the metaphor states, "I have some (spare) time on my hands," referring to the spare time a person has to do extra work.

This is the reality of time; what we can look at and what we are in, while we were writing and while you are reading this short message, the time is ticking away.

How would you make the most out of it? To begin with, plan your day in the morning. If you get used to it, then you know that at least your chores are being done in a systematic way and you are also heading in the right direction. The Holy Prophet ﷺ said "Two such blessings which are not valued by the people; health and spare time." (Bukhāri)

You had health and you stepped back. You had spare time and you stepped back. Then you say you were inflicted with something and/or you had so much work to do but time has ran away from you. Now you have left no time in your hands and now, you are running behind time as usual.

It is mentioned in the Holy Qur'ān,

"Closer to mankind comes their reckoning, yet they heedlessly turn away." (21:1)

The significance of time can be (indirectly) understood by the following two Ahādīth. The Holy Prophet ﷺ, whilst pointing with his middle and index fingers said, "The time space between my advent and the Final Hour is like these two fingers."

In another Hadīth of similar importance, the Holy Prophet ﷺ said, "The Hour almost came before me."

This sums it all up in terms of succeeding in the Hereafter and in terms of doing well in this world. It is totally up to the individual. The time is now to make use of your time. Take it at your disposal, take it at your discretion; there is simply no time to stick around.

Don't Waffle, Speak Clear

Ambiguity is the result of uncertainty and a lack of direction. A Muslim should be focused, resolute and dedicated to Allāh ﷻ with no time for wastage. Think before you act. Think before you speak. If in doubt, be silent and hold your peace. If you have something to say then say it clearly and concisely; don't just waffle!

My struggle with most people is that they do not speak clearly. Ambiguity makes me uneasy. Even if the matter is small it should be clear and concise. This is what is missing in most people. I try to instil this but (then) people get apprehensive. They want to conclude matters in a wishy-washy way as is done by the ignorant and pretentious person. I become uneasy when people speak in such a manner. I restrict them to which the entrants become perturbed. So this is my struggle. If one speaks clear, I have no complains.

(Shaykh Ashraf Ali Thānwi ﷺ)

How to Excel In Your Studies

Want to excel in your studies? Then look at those who excelled before you! Learn to inculcate and adopt their methods if you want to excel!

When you read the biographies or autobiographies of the esteemed scholars of Dārul Uloom, Deoband, then undoubtedly you will come to discover that each one of them was an exemplary model in his own right of Islamic knowledge whether it was external knowledge or internal knowledge (Tasawwuf). They set a standard for the next generation of Scholars. For example, Shaykh Ahmad Ali Lahori ؒ who was known as Shaykhut-Tafsīr (a master in Tafseer), Shaykh Ashraf Ali Thānwi ؒ who was known as Hakīmul Ummah; the spiritual physician of the Ummah, whose books alone, number to more than a thousand. Moreover, Shaykhul Hind, Maulāna Mahmūdul Hasan ؒ, a renowned Muhaddith and a political activist and the list continues.

Among those luminary scholars I would like to discuss, is a man who excelled his contemporaries and whose works have been accepted by worldwide scholars; Arab and non-Arab alike. One of his famous works is Awjaz-ul-Masālik (an 18 volume commentary on the Muwatta of Imām Mālik), an Arab scholar once said قَدْ حَنَّفَ الْمُوَطَّا meaning he has written such an outstanding commentary on Imām Mālik's ؒ book that it is as though Imām Mālik ؒ himself was a Hanafi! Only scholars can comprehend how much weight such a bold statement holds! This luminary scholar is the renowned Shaykh ul-Hadīth, Shaykh Muhammad Zakariyyā Ibn Shaykh Yahyā Muhājir Madani ﷺ.

The house of Shaykh Yahyā ﷺ (the father of Shaykh Zakariyyā ﷺ) was blessed with his birth on the 10th of Ramadhān 1315 AH (which corresponds with Wednesday 2nd February 1898).

Shaykh Zakariyyā ﷺ was blessed with the company of great scholars from a very young age. He was nurtured by Shaykh Rashīd Ahmad Gangohi ﷺ (co-founder of Dārul Uloom Deoband). No doubt that his blessed spiritual attention had a huge impact on Shaykh Zakariyyā's ﷺ spiritual upbringing and wellbeing. This, along with memorising the Noble Qur'ān under the supervision of his father and learning the elementary Persian books by his paternal uncle, Maulāna Ilyās ﷺ. Without a doubt, his household members were extremely religious and pious. It is reported that the womenfolk of his household used to complete an entire Qur'ān daily during the blessed month of Ramadhān whilst carrying out their household chores.

It would not be an overstatement to say that, if students of knowledge and scholars studied Shaykh Zakariyyā's ﷺ life and tried to emulate his examples, then institutes of Islamic knowledge will produce such scholars once again.

From a young age, his father brought Shaykh Zakariyyā ﷺ upon Islamic values. He embedded in him the qualities of the saints; sufficing with little, adopting moderation in clothing and food, sacrificing his time for the service of Dīn and studying and other saintly qualities. His father raised him on strict principles. Shaykh Zakariyyā ﷺ himself narrates in his autobiography that once, during his student days, in an attempt to emulate the pious scholars; he began to pray the Nawāfil prayers after Maghrib Salāh. His father, after seeing this, reprimanded him! He exclaimed "Why don't you learn your Sabaq (lessons)?!" At the time Shaykh Zakariyyā ﷺ became upset but then he came to realise that Shaytān, the accursed, can mislead a person by engaging him in optional acts of worship, thereby, distracting him from more important priorities.

Another lesson that can be learnt from this is that the elders (especially the scholars) have a deeper insight and wish for what is good; therefore, we should accept their advice and control our rebellious egos.

Shaykh Zakariyyā ﷺ spent a lot of time in the company of his spiritual mentor; Shaykh ul-Hadīth Maulāna Khalīl Ahmad Sahāranpūri ﷺ. Shaykh Zakariyyā ﷺ assisted his spiritual mentor in writing the infamous 20 volume commentary on the Sunan of Abū Dāwūd: Badhlul Majhūd fi Halli Sunan Abi Dawūd. Such an ocean of knowledge they both possessed!

Possessing immense amounts of knowledge is not the only factor which made Shaykh Zakariyyā ﷺ an extraordinary scholar; his piety, foresightedness and bestowal of knowledge (ilhām) were untouchable. His love for the leader of the two worlds, the Holy Prophet ﷺ was deeply immense, such that at times, he would fail to recognise his own son. After being in deep thought about the Holy Prophet ﷺ, he would stare at his son and ask, "Who are you?" Shaykh Talha would reply "It is Talha." This was as a result of his deep entrenched love for the Prophet Muhammad ﷺ; he would constantly be thinking about him.

As a result of this love, Allāh ﷺ took his soul in the beloved city of the Holy Prophet ﷺ, Madīnah Munawwarah. His soul departed on Monday, the 1st of Sha'bān, 1402 AH after Asr Salāh. The Janāzah Salāh took place in the blessed Masjid Nabawi after Ishā Salāh. To this day, he rests in the soil of Madīnah Munawwarah in the Baqī cemetery, near to where some of the Holy Prophet's ﷺ family members are buried. May Allāh ﷺ allow us to value and appreciate our pious predecessors and follow in their foot steps, Āmīn!

Every Deed Counts

That which is good when it is in your ability, then do it. Do not defer it or think low of it, as all good deeds done for the sake of Allāh ﷻ is great. That which is bad, avoid it at all costs as no disobedience against Allāh ﷻ is light if He so wishes to hold us to account.

One mistake which generally the careless make, is that they consider some good deeds to be lowly and do not save themselves from some deeds they know to be bad.

Some deeds are good but Shaytān misleads them by saying, 'The work that are most important, you do not do! So what is the worth of doing this good?' Similarly, sometime in regards to sins he says, 'You do not let go of the major sins. Having that, what is your piety worth?'

Remember! Do not consider any good deed as lowly, rather as soon as you have the ability, act upon it immediately. Nor, commit any sins thinking it to be small. In the Hadīth it has come that the Prophet of Allāh ﷺ said,

'O Āishah! Do not consider any good deeds as low for there is reward for it with Allāh and do not consider any bad deed as small for there is punishment for it with Allāh.'

Some people were forgiven due to a good deed without even realising it.

There is a story in the Hadīth, where there was a prostitute who was passing a jungle when she saw a dog dying of thirst. She felt sorry for this dog so she went to the well but there was no bucket or rope. She removed her leather socks, tied it to her scarf, removed water with it and fed it to the dog. This was the only good deed she done in her life and Allāh ﷻ forgave her on that action alone.

Some were forgiven due to removing a harmful item from the pathway. Imān has seventy odd branches. The finest of these is to say, 'There is none worthy of worship but Allāh' and the smallest is the removal of harm from the pathway.

Lifecycle of a Believer

Sūrah al-Asr is a fascinating Sūrah in the Qur'ān, despite it being the second shortest chapter, it sort of sets the details/blueprint and encompasses the cycle of a believer's life. Think about it.

"By the token of time. Indeed, mankind is in loss, except those who believe and do good deeds, and exhort one another to truth and exhort one another to patience." (Al-Asr)

A person's lifetime seems to follow a certain pattern: We are all in loss and in danger of losing our Hereafter – except for the believer. But when belief enters your heart, you naturally start doing deeds of righteousness. The moment you stand up for the Truth, is the time you will need to gather all the patience you can to overcome the obstacles that come in your way. This is because men and women of truth are tested and they are often fought by those who are still lingering in loss from amongst mankind … Subhān-Allāh.

It is no wonder that Imām Shāfi'ī 🕮 used to say, "If only this (Sūrah Al-Asr) was revealed, then it would suffice for mankind as guidance and righteousness."

Love for the Sake of Allāh ﷻ

Rasūlullāh ﷺ said,

"You will not enter Jannah until you believe and you will not believe until you love each other." (Muslim)

Two Types of Believers

Rasūlullāh ﷺ is addressing the believers in particular. He is telling the believers, if you want direct entry into Jannah without going into Jahannam you will need perfect faith which is only possible if one has love and affection. From this Hadīth we understand that there are two types of believers:

1. Perfect believers or complete believers
2. Imperfect believers or incomplete believers.

We should always strive to be perfect believers. As it is only a perfect believer that is guaranteed happiness and contentment in this world and the Hereafter.

An incomplete believer is not guaranteed peace in this world and nor at the time of death or in the grave and not on the Day of Judgement. We need to be perfect believers by striving to fulfill the commandments of Allāh ﷻ.

Our motto of our lives should be 'I can and I will'

Love for others

The Prophet ﷺ said,

> "A Muslim is a brother of another Muslim, he does not oppress him, he does not hand him over to an enemy. He will assist him and help him when he is in trouble."

In another Hadīth it states,

> "A Muslim will not deceive another Muslim, a Muslim will not lie to another Muslim."

In another Hadīth it says,

> "He will not look down upon him."

In one Hadīth it is mentioned,

> "Allāh's ﷻ help is with the servant as long as he is in the assistance of his brother."

Our love

How much love do we have for our brother? Our blood brother.

We don't love our brothers nor friends, we only love ourselves. That's why our friendship doesn't last for long. As long as their company gives us fun and enjoyment, we will be friends, but when they are of no help, then friendship is no more.

We change so many friends in our lives, either he will leave us or we will leave him because we are both selfish. We only have friendship for our self interests.

Love for Allāh ﷻ

Let us love our brothers for the sake of Allāh ﷻ.

Allāh ﷻ will say on the Day of Judgement, "Where are those who used to love each other for My pleasure, I will give them shade today under My shade when there is no shade."

The Love of the People of the Past

Abū Idrīs Al Khawlāni ؓ once went into the Masjid and saw Sayyidunā Mu'ādh Ibn Jabal ؓ, so he said to him,

"I love you for the sake of Allāh ﷻ."

He enquired, By Allāh you love me only for the sake of Allāh ﷻ?

Abū Idrīs 🕌 replied, "Yes."

Sayyidunā Mu'ādh Ibn Jabal 🕌 said: Receive glad tidings, for I have heard with my ears the Prophet 🕌 saying, "Allāh 🕌 says that those people who love each other for My pleasure, those people who sit with each other for My pleasure, those people who meet each other for My pleasure, those people who spend upon each other for My pleasure, My love is incumbent for them."

Once a person in Baghdad was overcome with debts. He approached an Ālim friend of his and requested if he could loan him some 400 Dīnārs. The Ālim friend went into his room where he kept the money and gave him the 400 Dīnārs after which the person went away. After his departure, the Ālim came into his house and started to weep profusely. His wife enquired: "Why are you crying? You just helped your friend and gave him 400 Dīnārs."

He replied: I am crying at my wretched state. I did not take care of the needs of my Muslim brother and was not aware of his needs. Due to this he was compelled to come and ask me. I should have been aware of his situation. I should have asked him if he needed anything so that he wouldn't need to come to ask me.

In another Hadīth it states, "Do not be jealous of each other, do not hate each other, do not turn away from one another and O' the servants of Allāh, be brothers."

The Holy Qur'ān states:

"Verily the believers are brothers" (49:10)

Live like brothers and love each other.

Another Hadīth states: "It is not permissible for a Muslim to stop talking to his brother for more than three days, if he stops talking for more than three days and passes away he will enter the fire." It was this love that inspired Sayyidunā Abū Bakr ﷺ to go in the villages and milk the goats of the widows during his Caliphate.

Key to love one another
Key to direct entry into Jannah is to be a complete believer and to be a complete believer, loving each other is necessary. In order to love each other, spread Salām amongst yourselves.

The Hadīth uses the word "spread" and not the word "say". Muhaddithūn say spread means,

1. Frequently
2. Do Salām loudly

Rasūlullāh ﷺ was once asked, 'Which are the best acts of Islām?'
1. You feed people
2. You do Salām to those who you are acquainted with and those who you are not acquainted with. (Those who you know and those who you don't know).

(Shaykh Muhammad Salīm Dhorāt Sāhib)

What is Taqwa?

Taqwa is when you miss a single prayer, you feel uneasy the entire day.

Taqwa is when you speak a lie, your instinct feels bad.

Taqwa is the guilt that follows when you hurt someone knowingly or unknowingly.

Taqwa is the shame and regret that follows a sin you did, knowing full well about its stand in the sight of Allāh ﷻ.

Taqwa is when you cannot sleep the whole night after disobeying or disrespecting your parents.

Taqwa is to cry in the depths of night fearing none but the Unseen One.
Taqwa is the fear that refrains us from sinning even when we are alone and nobody is looking.

Taqwa is the courage and the will to please Allāh ﷻ even when the whole world is engulfed in displeasing Him.

Taqwa is to stay happy and smiling even after knowing this world is a prison for believers.

Taqwa is the good manners and character that loving and fearing Allāh ﷻ brings in us.

Taqwa is the struggle to better yourself according to Islām with each passing of the day.

Taqwa is not only about rising in Dīn, it is more about falling but rising up again and never letting go.

Taqwa is unconditional love for Allāh ﷻ and His Prophet ﷺ.

Taqwa IS WHAT LIES IN THE HEART

When the heart is filled with Taqwa, then good actions automatically follow and you taste the sweetness of your good actions.

(Mahmūdul Hasan)

With Hardship Comes Ease

This is a message for anyone who is going through some difficulty in their life, be that in their marriage, at work, in their Dīn or anything else … Know that this life is not a place of absolute happiness or joy. There are ups and downs but Allāh ﷻ will never test you with more than you can handle. In His wisdom and justice He tests people according to their levels.

Know that the brightness of day follows the darkness of the night. So in your moment of darkness have glad tidings of the light which will follow and bear patiently with whatever comes in your way.

Some days it will seem like your back is against the wall and you can't go on, but don't you see how the bird flies for miles until it eventually reaches its food? The towering tree doesn't grow tall overnight - it sends its roots far and wide and then begins the slow, painful climb skywards. Likewise, your rise to the heights of Jannah won't be easy. Remain steadfast and focused until you reach your goal.

Yes, the road is long, the night is dark and lonely but know that whoever has Allāh ﷻ, then he has the ultimate Protector. To Allāh ﷻ belongs the treasures of the heavens and the earth. He gives them to whomever He Wills.

So I advise myself as well as yourself - keep your eye on the goal and keep moving towards it. The seas of life will get rocky and there will be storms, but in the morning perhaps there will be perfect stillness with no waves at all?

With hardship comes ease, with trials come rewards and with patience comes Jannah.

I am a Terrorist: Really?

I call myself a Muslim,
I have a long, thick beard,
I wear long clothes like Īsā رضى الله عنه, Mūsā رضى الله عنه and Muhammad ﷺ,
These were three men on the same mission, but
'I' am a terrorist.

I call myself a Muslimah,
I cover myself head to toe modestly, just like Mary (Mother of Jesus)
I reserve my body for my husband's eyes,
I do not show it off for promoting and advertising, but
'I' am a terrorist.

I follow the Prophetic way by washing my hands before I eat,
I am aware of cleanliness and hygiene,
I only eat that which Allāh ﷻ ordains Halāl,
I follow Allāh's ﷻ guidance and command, but
'I' am terrorist.

I work 9-5, to enjoy and spend my life,
With my family and friends and a beautiful wife,
I look after my body, eat healthy and go to the gym,
I love my Saturday night takeaway, but still try to look slim,
I try and live an ordinary life, make friends and mix in, but
'I' am a terrorist.

I pray five times a day, bowing and prostrating,
I pray to Allāh ﷻ to help us, each one and all,
I fast in Ramadhān, up to 18 hours without food and drink,
I help the poor by giving alms and charity, wherever they may be in
the world,
I promote unity and treating people fairly, but
'I' am a terrorist.

by
Ismāil Ibn Nazīr Sātia

Why Do People Leave Islām?

Is it because there is something wrong with Islām? Such people have never studied Islām properly and never practiced it entirely. Belief and faith is such that when it's sweetness enters the heart, then there is no turning back from it. The peace and tranquillity just keeps increasing as you practice. Lack of practice and excessive disobedience reduces this peace, to the extent that the person ends up in in confusion, disbelief, rejection and rebellion.

When we analyse those who left Islām, we see that, along with ignorance and lack of practice, people also leave Islām due to agitation, frustration and no proper guidance. But such people get angry over everything and upon everyone. It's like someone who is angry with the boss at the office, at the parents, teachers or at someone else with authority. They abandon them and then keep taking their anger out at them whenever and wherever they can. Such people can never be satisfied. We have to leave them as they are and move on.

Another reason, we notice in such people is pride and arrogance. They refuse to accept a good word of advice. They should learn to be humble and develop some humility. If they did have some humility, they would listen to their peers. They would try to find answers for any objections they might have had. We have plenty of learned people around. We have the technology. If they can't find any scholars in their vicinity, then they can do their own research on the net. And the best solution would be to make ablution, get on the prayer mat, pray and ask the Lord Almighty to inspire guidance in the heart, as it is He Who is the ultimate Guide. He inspires, He guides, and He talks to us in our hearts. He will surely guide a sincere seeker.

Haven't reverts to Islām suffered immensely enough previously? In fact there are reverts who have suffered much worse. Their parents kicked them out of the house. Their siblings disowned them. Their friends didn't want to know them. They were homeless. No job. No benefits to survive on. However they remained strong and moved on.

Then again, what is the aim of highlighting the cases of the apostates? It seems like they want others to do the same. So such programmes are in reality to advertise and promote this behaviour. The media will always find speakers who go into extreme, get carried away and say things which they would not normally say when they are calm. This is with politicians and others too. Why should they keep highlighting such remarks? Can they not find any good in Islām to talk about? Do we ever see on media the amazing charity work the Muslims do? Do we ever see a minute amount of the good that Muslims bring to this country?

How often do we here an ex-Muslim coming back to Islām? There is an incident where a woman after leaving Islām came back to it, because of the emptiness she felt after leaving Islām, she had no peace of mind, so she studied Islām properly with an open mind and started realising the beauty of Islām. She returned to Islām and this time with a better understanding of Islām.

There was once a student who left Islām and remained in that state for a few years. He read a book on Buddhism, which put the brakes on his belief that material world is everything, and that there is no such thing as spiritual life. The belief that we have to earn, eat, drink, sleep and enjoy our lives because 'you only live once, so make the most of it'. When he read the book, he realised that we don't just have the physical dimension but also a spiritual dimension. However, Buddhism only focuses on the spirituality which does not allow luxuries of life.

Then one of his friends gave him a copy of a good English translation of the Holy Qur'ān. He began to read it in his free time. Holy Qur'ān merges the physical and spiritual sides of our lives. Holy Qur'ān teaches us that we can enjoy our lives; however, we have to work on our spiritual dimension as well by praying, fasting, being charitable, invoking Allāh ﷻ and contemplating, etc. He now realised the reality. He found the answers in the Holy Qur'ān. It was as though God was talking to him directly and pointing out his mistakes and providing answers and solutions to his queries. Being a humble seeker of the truth, he reverted to Islām, went for further studies and became a great scholar of Dīn.

This individual who I am referring to is Shaykh Abdul Mājid Daryābādī ﷺ who wrote a beautiful Tafsīr of the Holy Qur'ān. May Allāh ﷻ guide us all towards the truth and keep us on the truth. May Allāh ﷻ forgive us and be pleased with us. Āmīn!

(Shaykh Abdur Rahīm Sāhib)

The Curious Case of Modern Muslims

Islām is a way of life, pivoted on guidelines derived from the Holy Qur'ān and Sunnah. Islām doesn't prevent man from quenching his needs, which include; hunger, thirst, marital relationship, socialising, gaining knowledge and shelter etc. all within a limited frame. Islām does not look at life in a pessimistic way; eternal bliss in the afterlife need not be achieved by suffering in this life.

The amusement and play of this life is temporary, but that doesn't mean everything that happens around is fake, joy exists, sorrow exists. Islām is about positive thinking. Islām teaches us what to do when facing life, challenging the odds and preparing ourselves to die with a weightless heart.

Islām encourages man to be fair to every part of his body, unlike what most people have interpreted today. Islām is not merely a bundle of customary and ritual practices such as wedding ceremonies, funerals, Friday prayers, fasting in Ramadhān and praying five times a day! People are confused about Islām, they have confined Islām to a few rituals only.

So what is this REAL Islām?
How many of us are trustworthy?
How many of us can keep secrets?
How many of us are truthful?
How many of us have measured speech? Do we even know what that

means?

How many of us are patient enough to bare insults?

How many of us are brave enough to stand up against oppression?

How many of us care about our neighbours? How many of us know that Muslims and Non-Muslims have a right over us and they will speak about us on the Day of Judgement?

How many of us know to tolerate the view point of another person?

How many of us give due respect to other religions before expecting them to respect us in return?

How many of us don't gossip?

How many of us practise the Hijāb, before telling the opposite sex to maintain it?

How many of us believe in true justice? Do we not favour a side or be biased at times?

How many of us know that cleanliness is half of Islām? How many Muslim homes, shops and Masājid are maintained that way?

How many of us respect the elders and love the young ones?

How many of us have got together and helped a person get out of his problems?

How many of us take weddings in a modest way?

How many of us care about the beggars in the streets? And how many of us are aware .

How many of us smile at the wayfarers we meet?

How many of us give Salām to others? Even if we do, I wonder whether we really know the meaning of what we just said?

How many of us are not enslaved to emotions and the material world?

How many of us are an example to the society and to our friends? How many of us are the "Khayrul-Ummah"? (Best of Nations- referring to the Muslims).

How many of us are united?

How many of us think positive and take what is good from what we hear rather than criticising the imperfections?

How many of us plant trees and cultivate the land?

That's about 20 points, and how much did you score?

Decades ago, Islām flourished and grew rapidly because people were practicing REAL ISLĀM!

Centuries ago, it was better; today some countries are having Tom, Dick and Harry implementing Sharī'ah. They have mixed laws of other religions and laws of their own with Islām, but when Muslims ruled Spain, when the Caliphs of the beginning were ruling, it was totally different.

How would we expect our non-Muslim brethren to care about what we preach, when even we and our own Muslim brothers and sisters don't practise it? It'll look like reading some bed time story book (probably Superman or Spiderman) to a child - WHY? Because we talk about this extremely pious life and the pinnacle of purity and don't act upon it, so it looks very hard and very theoretical and not practical!

Our beloved Prophet ﷺ was the most successful Prophet because he always practiced what he preached. Islām is perfect, there is no argument in that, even from an atheist's perspective. Islām is a superb way of maintaining law and order, maintaining a healthy quality of life, economy etc.

But without practising it, there is no effect in doing Da'wah! The easiest way to practise Islām properly is by associating with the right crowd. Islām is very easy to practice. This doesn't mean you have to abandon your friends who aren't Muslims, but it means, you need to gradually reduce the time you spend in idle talk and Fitnah!

Muhammad Wazim Akram, Sri Lanka

Sympathy or Sin?

A man was once mentioning the close friendship he had with his neighbour. In explaining their good relationship, their mutual understanding and support of each other he said, "The department in which my neighbour works offers many benefits for the convenience of their staff. They give free petrol, service, etc. to their staff to use for their cars. Now, my neighbour doesn't own a car, so he is unable to benefit from all these benefits. Since I have a car, I have registered the car on his name, so that he can claim the company benefits for the car. The company assumes the car to be his so they grant him the relevant benefits. This has been the case for years now."

When he was asked why they did this, he replied, "Our relationship is such. I knew that even though I registered the car on his name, I would still use it and there would be no problems in this regard between us. If by just registering a car on someone else's name there are so many benefits, why should I not take advantage of it?"

Another person once explained his friendship thus, "We have such a good relationship that if he or anyone in his home gets ill, then I get medicine for them on my name, because my company's medical aid pays for it and my friend does not have to pay anything for it."

Both of them have explained their friendship very proudly that seemingly signifies openness and generosity. They explain their deeds with such high regard that they are deserving of tremendous reward in both this world and the Hereafter.

Yet little do them both realise that through their mutual 'support and sympathy,' for one another in this manner, they are abusing the trust and wealth of their respective company. Such sympathy and 'generosity' entails in speaking lies. In the first instance, the owner of the car falsely placed the car on his neighbour's name and to which every month, the neighbour is falsely claiming benefits such as free petrol from the company. The car was in fact used by the real owner and the other person had to engage in lies year after year.

In the second case, the friend who bought the medicine on his name had to speak a lie to acquire the medicine and then he also had to involve the doctor in this lie to prescribe the medicine falsely for him, whilst he was in no need for it. This is also considered a breach of trust and a lie.

If the company devises a benefit system that is restricted to its staff members only, then one cannot personally extend it to his own family and friends, especially if one knows that the company will strongly disapprove of it. These benefits which the neighbour and friend had acquired and 'devised' are clearly Harām and impermissible. They are guilty of committing a sin. It is a complete misconception that they are doing good deeds which are worthy of reward.

These were just two examples. However, if we look around us, we will see many such examples where people abuse the benefit services and wealth of companies, employers etc.

Wherever any company awards any benefit for their staff, then these benefits are squeezed to their fullest by the staff and in many instances wrongfully. This requires lying, breaking the rules and general codes and defrauding.

On the other hand, some companies grant their staff a certain allowances for rent. Now the staff member may get a place to rent which is less than what the company allocates for him, he makes up a bill to give to the company where he gets the full amount allocated for him. The same is done with many other company allowances, like the medical bills, etc. where the staff don't genuinely use the allocated share, but they use medical bills etc. to claim extra from their companies.

All these actions are very low and distasteful in Dīn. In all such instances, there is a Shar'ī principle, which many people including religious people ignore. That principle is, the ownership of something and its usage are two different things. Something that belongs to you is for you to use however you wish but something that belongs to someone else is not your property to be used in the first place. If the owner, allows you to benefit from his property and no one else, you cannot take it in your hands in extending it to whomever you wish.

A simple example of this is that assuming someone cooked some food and sent it to your house. This food now becomes your property. Whether we eat the food, feed it to someone else or give it in Sadaqah, all this would be permissible because you are the owner now. In fact, it would also be permissible for us to sell that food and take the money. However, if someone invites you to his house to eat, then whatever food is present, it is not your property. There is, nevertheless, consent from the owner (host) that we eat as much as we wish. We cannot regard this food as our property, so we cannot invite someone else to also eat there (without the consent of the host).

It is unfortunate that many people nowadays do not regard this act as sinful, in actual fact they deem it their right (to claim for what they did not use) even though this entails lies and deceit.

The underlying cause for all this is that people nowadays have made money and worldly belongings their objective in life because of which they start deceiving others. This condition is not expected to change overnight, but that does not mean that we remain the way we are and make no effort to make right the wrongs we are currently involved in. Good character and a Dīni (religious) environment are like perfume, which eventually reaches every corner. Even the fumes of bad habits effect its surrounding.

Other titles from JKN Publications

Your Questions Answered

An outstanding book written by Shaykh Mufti Saiful Islām. A very comprehensive yet simple Fatāwa book and a source of guidance that reaches out to a wider audience i.e. the English speaking Muslims. The reader will benefit from the various answers to questions based on the Laws of Islām relating to the beliefs of Islām, knowledge, Sunnah, pillars of Islām, marriage, divorce and contemporary issues.

UK RRP: £7.50

Hadeeth for Beginners

A concise Hadeeth book with various Ahādeeth that relate to basic Ibādāh and moral etiquettes in Islām accessible to a wider readership. Each Hadeeth has been presented with the Arabic text, its translation and commentary to enlighten the reader, its meaning and application in day-to-day life.

UK RRP: £3.00

Du'ā for Beginners

This book contains basic Du'ās which every Muslim should recite on a daily basis. Highly recommended to young children and adults studying at Islamic schools and Madrasahs so that one may cherish the beautiful treasure of supplications of our beloved Prophet ﷺ in one's daily life, which will ultimately bring peace and happiness in both worlds, Inshā-Allāh.

UK RRP: £2.00

How well do you know Islām?

An exciting educational book which contains 300 multiple questions and answers to help you increase your knowledge on Islām! Ideal for the whole family, especially children and adult students to learn new knowledge in an enjoyable way and cherish the treasures of knowledge that you will acquire from this book. A very beneficial tool for educational syllabus.

UK RRP: £3.00

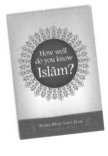

Treasures of the Holy Qur'ān

This book entitled "Treasures of the Holy Qur'ān" has been compiled to create a stronger bond between the Holy Qur'ān and the readers. It mentions the different virtues of Sūrahs and verses from the Holy Qur'ān with the hope that the readers will increase their zeal and enthusiasm to recite and inculcate the teachings of the Holy Qur'ān into their daily lives.

UK RRP: £3.00

Marriage - A Complete Solution

Islām regards marriage as a great act of worship. This book has been designed to provide the fundamental teachings and guidelines of all what relates to the marital life in a simplified English language. It encapsulates in a nutshell all the marriage laws mentioned in many of the main reference books in order to facilitate their understanding and implementation.

UK RRP: £5.00

Pearls of Luqmān

This book is a comprehensive commentary of Sūrah Luqmān, written beautifully by Shaykh Mufti Saiful Islām. It offers the reader with an enquiring mind, abundance of advice, guidance, counselling and wisdom.

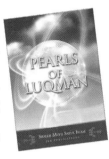

The reader will be enlightened by many wonderful topics and anecdotes mentioned in this book, which will create a greater understanding of the Holy Qur'ān and its wisdom. The book highlights some of the wise sayings and words of advice Luqmān ﷺ gave to his son.

UK RRP: £3.00

Arabic Grammar for Beginners

This book is a study of Arabic Grammar based on the subject of Nahw (Syntax) in a simplified English format. If a student studies this book thoroughly, he/she will develop a very good foundation in this field, Inshā-Allāh. Many books have been written on this subject in various languages such as Arabic, Persian and Urdu. However, in this day and age there is a growing demand for this subject to be available in English .

UK RRP: £3.00

A Gift to My Youngsters

This treasure filled book, is a collection of Islamic stories, morals and anecdotes from the life of our beloved Prophet ﷺ, his Companions ﷺ and the pious predecessors. The stories and anecdotes are based on moral and ethical values, which the reader will enjoy sharing with their peers, friends, families and loved ones.

"A Gift to My Youngsters" – is a wonderful gift presented to the readers personally, by the author himself, especially with the youngsters in mind. He has carefully selected stories and anecdotes containing beautiful morals, lessons and valuable knowledge and wisdom.

UK RRP: £5.00

Travel Companion

The beauty of this book is that it enables a person on any journey, small or distant or simply at home, to utilise their spare time to read and benefit from an exciting and vast collection of important and interesting Islamic topics and lessons. Written in simple and easy to read text, this book will immensely benefit both the newly interested person in Islām and the inquiring mind of a student expanding upon their existing knowledge. Inspiring reminders from the Holy Qur'ān and the blessed words of our beloved Prophet ﷺ beautifies each topic and will illuminate the heart of the reader. **UK RRP: £5.00**

Pearls of Wisdom

Junaid Baghdādi ﷺ once said, "Allāh ﷻ strengthens through these Islamic stories the hearts of His friends, as proven from the Qur'anic verse,
"And all that We narrate unto you of the stories of the Messengers, so as to strengthen through it your heart." (11:120)
Mālik Ibn Dinār ﷺ stated that such stories are gifts from Paradise. He also emphasised to narrate these stories as much as possible as they are gems and it is possible that an individual might find a truly rare and invaluable gem among them. **UK RRP: £6.00**

Inspirations

This book contains a compilation of selected speeches delivered by Shaykh Mufti Saiful Islām on a variety of topics such as the Holy Qur'ān, Nikāh and eating Halāl. Having previously been compiled in separate booklets, it was decided that the transcripts be gathered together in one book for the benefit of the reader. In addition to this, we have included in this book, further speeches which have not yet been printed.

UK RRP: £6.00

Gift to my Sisters

A thought provoking compilation of very interesting articles including real life stories of pious predecessors, imaginative illustrations and much more. All designed to influence and motivate mothers, sisters, wives and daughters towards an ideal Islamic lifestyle. A lifestyle referred to by our Creator, Allāh ﷻ in the Holy Qur'ān as the means to salvation and ultimate success.

UK RRP: £6.00

Gift to my Brothers

A thought provoking compilation of very interesting articles including real life stories of pious predecessors, imaginative illustrations, medical advices on intoxicants and rehabilitation and much more. All designed to influence and motivate fathers, brothers, husbands and sons towards an ideal Islamic lifestyle. A lifestyle referred to by our Creator, Allāh ﷻ in the Holy Qur'ān as the means to salvation and ultimate success.

UK RRP: £5.00

Heroes of Islam

"In the narratives there is certainly a lesson for people of intelligence (understanding)." (12:111)

A fine blend of Islamic personalities who have been recognised for leaving a lasting mark in the hearts and minds of people.

A distinguishing feature of this book is that the author has selected not only some of the most world and historically famous renowned scholars but also these lesser known and a few who have simply left behind a valuable piece of advice to their nearest and dearest.

UK RRP: £5.00

Ask a Mufti (3 volumes)

Muslims in every generation have confronted different kinds of challenges. In-spite of that, Islām produced such luminary Ulamā who confronted and re-sponded to the challenges of their time to guide the Ummah to the straight path. "Ask A Mufti" is a comprehensive three volume fatwa book, based on the Hanafi School, covering a wide range of topics related to every aspect of human life such as belief, ritual worship, life after death and contemporary legal topics related to purity, commercial transaction, marriage, divorce, food, cosmetic, laws pertaining to women, Islamic medical ethics and much more.

UK RRP: £30.00

Should I Follow a Madhab?

Taqleed or following one of the four legal schools is not a new phenomenon. Historically, scholars of great calibre and luminaries, each one being a specialist in his own right, were known to have adhered to one of the four legal schools. It is only in the previous century that a minority group emerged advocating a se-vere ban on following one of the four major schools.

This book endeavours to address the topic of Taqleed and elucidates its im-portance and necessity in this day and age. It will also, by the Divine Will of Allāh ﷻ dispel some of the confusion surrounding this topic.

UK RRP: £5.00

Advice for the Students of Knowledge

Allāh ﷻ describes divine knowledge in the Holy Qur'ān as a 'Light'. Amongst the qualities of light are purity and guidance. The Holy Prophet ﷺ has clearly ex-plained this concept in many blessed Ahādeeth and has also taught us many supplications in which we ask for beneficial knowledge.

This book is a golden tool for every sincere student of knowledge wishing to mould his/her character and engrain those correct qualities in order to be wor-thy of receiving the great gift of Ilm from Allāh ﷻ.

UK RRP: £3.00

Stories for Children

"Stories for Children" - is a wonderful gift presented to the readers personally by the author himself, especially with the young children in mind. The stories are based on moral and ethical values, which the reader will enjoy sharing with their peers, friends, families and loved ones. The aim is to present to the children stories and incidents which contain moral lessons, in order to reform and correct their lives, according to the Holy Qur'ān and Sunnah.

UK RRP: £5.00

Pearls from My Shaykh

This book contains a collection of pearls and inspirational accounts of the Holy Prophet ﷺ, his noble Companions, pious predecessors and some personal accounts and sayings of our well-known contemporary scholar and spiritual guide, Shaykh Mufti Saiful Islām Sāhib. Each anecdote and narrative of the pious predecessors have been written in the way that was narrated by Mufti Saiful Islām Sāhib in his discourses, drawing the specific lessons he intended from telling the story. The accounts from the life of the Shaykh has been compiled by a particular student based on their own experience and personal observation. **UK RRP: £5.00**

Paradise & Hell

This book is a collection of detailed explanation of Paradise and Hell including the state and conditions of its inhabitants. All the details have been taken from various reliable sources. The purpose of its compilation is for the reader to contemplate and appreciate the innumerable favours, rewards, comfort and unlimited luxuries of Paradise and at the same time take heed from the punishment of Hell. Shaykh Mufti Saiful Islām Sāhib has presented this book in a unique format by including the Tafseer and virtues of Sūrah Ar-Rahmān. **UK RRP: £5.00**

Prayers for Forgiveness

Prayers for Forgiveness' is a short compilation of Du'ās in Arabic with English translation and transliteration. This book can be studied after 'Du'ā for Beginners' or as a separate book. It includes twenty more Du'ās which have not been mentioned in the previous Du'ā book. It also includes a section of Du'ās from the Holy Qur'ān and a section from the Ahādeeth. The book concludes with a section mentioning the Ninety-Nine Names of Allāh ﷻ with its translation and transliteration. **UK RRP: £3.00**

Scattered Pearls

This book is a collection of scattered pearls taken from books, magazines, emails and WhatsApp messages. These pearls will hopefully increase our knowledge, wisdom and make us realise the purpose of life. In this book, Mufti Sāhib has included messages sent to him from scholars, friends and colleagues which will be beneficial and interesting for our readers Inshā-Allāh. **UK RRP: £4.00**

Poems of Wisdom

This book is a collection of poems from those who contributed to the Al-Mumin Magazine in the poems section. The Hadeeth mentions "Indeed some form of poems are full of wisdom." The themes of each poem vary between wittiness, thought provocation, moral lessons, emotional to name but a few. The readers will benefit from this immensely and make them ponder over the outlook of life in general.

UK RRP: £4.00

Horrors of Judgement Day
This book is a detailed and informative commentary of the first three Sūrahs of the last Juz namely; Sūrah Naba, Sūrah Nāzi'āt and Sūrah Abasa. These Sūrahs vividly depict the horrific events and scenes of the Great Day in order to warn mankind the end of this world. These Sūrahs are an essential reminder for us all to instil the fear and concern of the Day of Judgement and to detach ourselves from the worldly pleasures. Reading this book allows us to attain the true realization of this world and provides essential advices of how to gain eternal salvation in the Hereafter.

RRP: £5:00

Spiritual Heart
It is necessary that Muslims always strive to better themselves at all times and to free themselves from the destructive maladies. This book focusses on three main spiritual maladies; pride, anger and evil gazes. It explains its root causes and offers some spiritual cures. Many examples from the lives of the pious predecessors are used for inspiration and encouragement for controlling the above three maladies. It is hoped that the purification process of the heart becomes easy once the underlying roots of the above maladies are clearly understood. **UK RRP: £5:00**

Hajj & Umrah for Beginners
This book is a step by step guide on Hajj and Umrah for absolute beginners. Many other additional important rulings (Masāil) have been included that will Insha-Allāh prove very useful for our readers. The book also includes some etiquettes of visiting (Ziyārat) of the Holy Prophet's ﷺ blessed Masjid and his Holy Grave.

UK RRP £3:00

Advice for the Spiritual Travellers
This book contains essential guidelines for a spiritual Murīd to gain some familiarity of the science of Tasawwuf. It explains the meaning and aims of Tasawwuf, some understanding around the concept of the soul, and general guidelines for a spiritual Murīd. This is highly recommended book and it is hoped that it gains wider readership among those Murīds who are basically new to the science of Tasawwuf.

UK RRP £3:00

Don't Worry Be Happy
This book is a compilation of sayings and earnest pieces of advice that have been gathered directly from my respected teacher Shaykh Mufti Saiful Islām Sāhib. The book consists of many valuable enlightenments including how to deal with challenges of life, promoting unity, practicing good manners, being optimistic and many other valuable advices. Our respected Shaykh has gathered this Naseehah from meditating, contemplating, analysing and searching for the gems within Qur'anic verses, Ahādeeth and teachings of our Pious Predecessors. **UK RRP £1:00**

Kanzul Bāri

Kanzul Bāri provides a detailed commentary of the Ahādeeth contained in Saheeh al-Bukhāri. The commentary includes Imām Bukhāri's ﷺ biography, the status of his book, spiritual advice, inspirational accounts along with academic discussions related to Fiqh, its application and differences of opinion. Moreover, it answers objections arising in one's mind about certain Ahādeeth. Inquisitive students of Hadeeth will find this commentary a very useful reference book in the final year of their Ālim course for gaining a deeper understanding of the science of Hadeeth.   **UK RRP: £15.00**

How to Become a Friend of Allāh ﷺ

The friends of Allāh ﷺ have been described in detail in the Holy Qur'ān and Āhadeeth. This book endeavours its readers to help create a bond with Allāh ﷺ in attaining His friendship as He is the sole Creator of all material and immaterial things. It is only through Allāh's ﷺ friendship, an individual will achieve happiness in this life and the Hereafter, hence eliminate worries, sadness, depression, anxiety and misery of this world.   **UK RRP: £3.00**

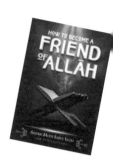

Gems & Jewels

This book contains a selection of articles which have been gathered for the benefit of the readers covering a variety of topics on various aspects of daily life. It offers precious advice and anecdotes that contain moral lessons. The advice captivates its readers and will extend the narrowness of their thoughts to deep reflection, wisdom and appreciation of the purpose of our existence.

UK RRP: £4.00

End of Time

This book is a comprehensive explanation of the three Sūrahs of Juzz Amma; Sūrah Takweer, Sūrah Infitār and Sūrah Mutaffifeen. This book is a continuation from the previous book of the same author, 'Horrors of Judgement Day'. The three Sūrahs vividly sketch out the scene of the Day of Judgement and describe the state of both the inmates of Jannah and Jahannam. Mufti Saiful Islām Sāhib provides an easy but comprehensive commentary of the three Sūrahs facilitating its understanding for the readers whilst capturing the horrific scene of the ending of the world and the conditions of mankind on that horrific Day.   **UK RRP: £5.00**

Andalus (modern day Spain), the long lost history, was once a country that produced many great calibre of Muslim scholars comprising of Mufassirūn, Muhaddithūn, Fuqahā, judges, scientists, philosophers, surgeons, to name but a few. The Muslims conquered Andalus in 711 AD and ruled over it for eight-hundred years. This was known as the era of Muslim glory. Many non-Muslim Europeans during that time travelled to Spain to study under Muslim scholars. The remanences of the Muslim rule in Spain are manifested through their universities, magnificent palaces and Masājid carved with Arabic writings, standing even until today. In this book, Shaykh Mufti Saiful Islām shares some of his valuable experiences he witnessed during his journey to Spain.   **UK RRP: £3.00**